Social Trends in Education

Editor
Dr. Vinod V. Patil
Associate Professor
Dr. M. H. A. College of Education,
Malegaon (Nashik)

Title   : Social Trends in Education

Author   : Dr. Vinod V. Patil

Edition   : First (June, 2024)

ISBN   : 9788197950544

Published by

PRACHI
DIGITAL PUBLICATION

Regd. Add.: 254, Khuriyakhatta No. 10, Bindukhatta,
Lalkuan, Nainital - 262402, Uttarakhand, India
Website : www.prachidigital.com
E-mail : info@prachidigital.in
Phone : +91 976041 7980, +91 976041 8103

Printed by :

Manipal Technologies Limited, Bengaluru - 560001, Karnataka

INDEX

CHAPTER ONE

THE LEGAL AND SOCIAL DIMENSIONS OF FORCED MARRIAGES IN INDIA: A STUDY

Mr. Baban T. Bhalerao,
Assistant Professor,
N. B. Thakur Law College,
Nashik-05

ABSTRACT

We respect marriage as a holy bond that unites two people and endures a lifetime. There is now a platonic as well as physical tie. It is said that marriage affects both the body and the mind. However, certain social pressures erode this sacred bond by establishing legal and social violations such as forced, early, and child marriage. These elements erode the fundamental goal of marriage and make the couple's dissolution worse. In India, child marriages and forced marriages are commonplace. Despite India's tremendous progress, forced and child marriages are still common in many areas of the nation. The present study is related to the social and legal dimensions of forced marriages. The first objective of the study is to understand the concept of forced marriages with different approaches. The second objective of the study is to discuss the law relating to forced Marriages. The third objective of the study is to various dimensions of forced marriages. In this chapter, the researcher has focused on human trafficking for forced marriages and also another purpose of forced marriages is slavery.

Keywords: Forced Marriages, Social Dimension of forced Marriages, Legal Dimensions of Forced Marriages, Forced Marriages for Slavery, Forced Marriage is a Form of Human Trafficking.

INTRODUCTION

We honour marriage as a sacred union that lasts a lifetime and brings two people together. Both a physical and platonic bond has been formed. It is believed that marriage has an impact on the mind and body. But some social pressures tarnish this sacred connection by creating social and legal transgressions including child, young, and forced marriage. These factors weaken the foundational purpose of marriage and exacerbate the disintegration of the couple's union. Forced marriages and child weddings are frequent in India. In many parts of India, forced and child marriages continue to be prevalent despite the country's rapid development.

Forced, child, and early marriage is a harmful custom that infringes upon human rights, disproportionately impacting women and girls globally and making it impossible for them to live free from all forms of abuse. Data from UNICEF (2018) indicates that 12 million girls get married before they turn eighteen each year. That's equivalent to one in five girls globally, whose childhoods end too soon and whose future possibilities are compromised. A marriage is deemed forced if the couple is incapable of making any of those choices, such as when they are coerced emotionally or psychologically because they believe they will bring shame to their family, or when they are physically forced to marry because of threats, physical abuse, or sexual harassment. Based on data given by the UK Home Office, India was one of the top four countries in which the UK focused on forced marriages in 2017. Furthermore, while child marriage is forbidden in India, young girls under the age of eighteen are forced into marriages.

Women must understand their legal rights and other options outside of forced marriage. It is not just for women. In places like Bihar, forced marriages, commonly referred to as "Pakadua Shaadi," are a long-standing tradition. In Bihar, seven eligible bachelors are kidnapped and forced into marriage every day on average. Thus, every year, 1500–1800 marriages take place. The basic concept of the ritual is to abscond from the bride's family with an exorbitant demand for dowry; in modern times, this is achieved by abducting brides and forcing them into marriage with worthy grooms.

CONCEPT AND DEFINITION OF FORCED MARRIAGES

"When pressure or abuse is used to force a marriage between one or both parties—or, in the instance of someone with a learning disability, neither of them can consent—it is referred to as a forced marriage. It is an abhorrent and inexcusable practice that is acknowledged in the UK as a significant violation of human rights, domestic and child abuse, and violence against both men and women.

People may be under physical, emotional, or psychological pressure to marry against their will. Physical pressure includes threats, actual physical abuse, and sexual violence. Psychological pressure includes making someone feel like they're betraying their family. Financial abuse can also include having your wages taken from you or not receiving any money at all."[1]

Forced marriages are defined as unions that take place against the will of the parties involved or that they have agreed to but have not yet finalized.

In addition to abuse or harassment of the emotions and psychological processes, the term "force" also refers to compulsion that is social, psychological, physical, or emotional.

Forced marriage describes circumstances where a person feels coerced to the point of consenting, but only because they feel they have no other option and wouldn't have consented if the pressure hadn't been applied.

Additionally, women and girls discuss how they had a "feeling" or even just "knowing" that they would be beaten physically, shunned, or told by their family that they brought dishonor to the marriage, should they attempt to delay getting married.

This study on forced marriages aims to explain the problems in terms of the federal government and link federal aspects to the problem by talking about the role of patriarchy. This method can provide fresh perspectives and useful elements for next studies. The issues of humiliation, guilt, causes, effects, factors, the role of patriarchy, limitations, remedies, and ways to resolve forced marriages in different states are discussed.

Therefore, a "forced" or "constrained" marriage is one in which at least one of the parties is married without their permission or against their will. It can also become constrained if one or both feel

---

[1] 'Forced Marriage and the Law' (*Rights of Women*) <https://rightsofwomen.org.uk/get-information/family-law/forced-marriage-law/> accessed 7 May 2020.

'compelled' to continue in the marriage against their will, even if both parties enter it willingly. On the other hand, an organized marriage is one in which the partners supposedly agree to have their parents or a third party, such a relational arranger, help them choose and locate a mate. Various sorts of intimidation, ranging from overt physical aggression to subtle psychological strain, frequently target a marriage.

Large money offers or threats of violence against their families or lives were most often used to seal forced marriages. Unlike other states, Bihar is known for its patriarchal culture, and the dowry system has become a profitable business for the parents of eligible bachelors. Girls stay single because their parents are unable to pay the expectations of these grooms.[2]

Forced marriages were typically consummated with substantial money offers or threats of harm against their families or lives. Unlike other states, Bihar has a traditionally patriarchal society, and the parents of eligible bachelors have made a lot of money from the dowry system. Girls stay unmarried because their parents are unable to pay these grooms' expectations.

Forced Marriages for Slavery

Before designating forced marriage as human trafficking, the UN considered it to be a kind of slavery.

According to Article 1 of the Slavery Convention of 1926, "the

---

[2] chrome-extension://efaidnbmnnnibpcajpcglclefindmkaj/https://www.girlsnotbrides.org/documents/1539/FINAL-CB_India_ChildMarriageReport_Mar-4-2021.pdf

status or condition of a person over whom any or all of the powers attaching to the right of ownership are exercised" is defined as slavery.

The world slave trade had been essentially outlawed since the 1926 convention, but slavery-like institutions persisted, according to the 1956 Supplementary Convention on the Abolition of Slavery, the Slave Trade, and Institutions and Practices Similar to Slavery, which was held 60 years later.[3]

FORCED MARRIAGE IS A FORM OF HUMAN TRAFFICKING

Ratified by the UN in November 2000, the Protocol was the first legally binding agreement that included an internationally recognized definition of human trafficking. Forced marriage is considered human trafficking under the Protocol because it gives one person the power to exploit another, possibly through forced labor or services, slavery, or acts that are similar to slavery or servitude.

The Protocol's concept of human trafficking satisfies the definition of slavery, which includes forced marriage. The term is far more inclusive when children are included. Getting a kid to use them for personal gain is known as human trafficking. In this context, anyone under the age of eighteen is regarded as a child.[4]

Social Dimensions of Forced Marriages:

We need to consider the social norms surrounding forced marriages to fully understand their social dimension. Social norms are guidelines for what constitutes appropriate behavior for members of a community. Socially acceptable norms are the

---

3 https://theexodusroad.com/forced-marriage-and-human-trafficking/
4 Ibid

standards of behavior that are accepted in every culture. People who behave differently from other members of the society and defy societal standards are generally viewed as abnormal and may suffer disciplinary action, legal action, or social exclusion.

A family is established through marriage, which is one of the social institutions that keeps it alive. In contemporary society, most marriages occur with the mutual permission of the bride and groom, or their families. However, a wealth of evidence also suggests that forced marriages of women particularly minors occur without the will or consent of the parties involved. Getting married to a woman without her will and permission is not only against societal norms but also a criminal offense and a grave violation of her human rights.[5]

LEGAL DIMENSIONS OF FORCED MARRIAGES:

Forced marriage is directed gender violence as well as an infringement on fundamental rights. An individual's fundamental rights are violated when forced against their will, as stated in Articles 14, 19, and 21 of the Indian Constitution. No one shall be deprived of their life or freedom, as stated in Article 21 of the Indian Constitution. This provision also guarantees the right to life and liberty, which includes the freedom for all parties to a marriage to freely and fully consent to it. In India, it comes with the benefit of voluntary marriage. In fact, according to the law, a marriage is only

---

[5] chrome-

extension://efaidnbmnnnibpcajpcglclefindmkaj/https://satyarthi.org.in/wp-content/uploads/2022/12/Forced-Brides-in-India.pdf

considered legitimate if both parties freely consent to it; otherwise, it becomes void.

Any use of force against women is subject to the IPC's Section 350 legal provisions. Furthermore, Section 15 of the Indian Contract Act of 1872 can be applied in this same manner. A woman may be forced into marriage against her will or without getting legal approval, which renders the agreement void. The agreement that was made under duress is not enforceable in court. Matrimony is a social contract that is nullified if any party uses compulsion to get the other party's assent. In the same way, women who are coerced into marriage are subject to section 366 of the Indian Penal Code.

The Indian Judicial System gives women the power and ability to lodge a complaint against her own family, relatives, or anybody else who is pressuring her into marriage against her will and infringing upon her rights and freedoms as a result.

The Universal Declaration of Human Rights addresses discrimination against women in topics pertaining to marriage in Article 16. Similarly, Article 16 of the UDHR states that marriage is a social compact that can only be entered into with the free and informed consent of both parties. It guarantees that men and women have the same, unalienable right to marry and select a mate with their free and informed consent. As to Article 23 of the 1966 International Covenant on Civil and Political Rights, a marriage cannot take place unless the intending spouses provide their free and informed permission. These rules protect those who are victims of forced marriages and apply to all people, regardless of gender.[6]

There are various laws available for the protection of people

---

[6] Ibid

against forced and child marriages. These include:

The Prohibition of Child Marriage Act, 2006 (

The Guardians and Wards Act, 1890

The Majority Act, 1875

The Family Courts Act, 1984

Protection of Women from Domestic Violence Act, 2005

CONCLUSION

The individual who is the target of such an act has legal recourse thanks to the laws. The person now has the authority to take severe legal action against anyone who pressures him into a not-expected marriage. It is up to him to file a lawsuit against whoever is pressuring him; therefore, it depends on whether he will use this power or not. However, since these individuals are typically the person's parents or guardians, he finds it difficult to take any action against them. Since India is still a developing nation where people are still not accustomed to modern thinking, acting against one's parents is still seen as morally repugnant. One of the biggest abuses of human rights is forced marriage, which can lead to a host of other social ills such as marital rape, domestic abuse, and psychological and emotional abuse. To stop forced marriages, rules that are stricter and raise greater awareness are needed.

Besides stringent laws to protect women from forced marriages, it is my observation there are some areas in Jalgaon and Nashik District in the Maharashtra state and Burahanpur District in Madhya Pradesh where parents are selling their daughters in Gujrat and Rajasthan with the support of agents. And no one can file a complaint against them because of the involvement of the families in that menace.

REFERENCES:

1. chrome-extension://efaidnbmnnnibpcajpcglclefindmkaj/https://www.girlsnotbrides.org/documents/1539/FINAL-CB_India_ChildMarriageReport_Mar-4-2021.pdf

2. chrome-extension://efaidnbmnnnibpcajpcglclefindmkaj/https://epgp.inflibnet.ac.in/epgpdata/uploads/epgp_content/S001610/P001769/M023973/ET/1507527648Mod34humantraffickingandforcedmarriagesinindiatext.pdf

3. https://www.researchgate.net/publication/374902492_Understanding_Custom_of_Forced_Marriages_An_Exploratory_Study_of_Bihar/link/6534e75a1d6e8a7070443516/download?_tp=eyJjb250ZXh0Ijp7ImZpcnN0UGFnZSI6InB1YmxpY2F0aW9uIiwicGFnZSI6InB1YmxpY2F0aW9uIn19

4. chrome-extension://efaidnbmnnnibpcajpcglclefindmkaj/https://www.ijfmr.com/papers/2023/5/7568.pdf

5. chrome-extension://efaidnbmnnnibpcajpcglclefindmkaj/https://satyarthi.org.in/wp-content/uploads/2022/12/Forced-Brides-in-India.pdf

6. chrome-extension://efaidnbmnnnibpcajpcglclefindmkaj/https://patnawomenscollege.in/upload/Explore%20vol%20XI%202/detal/d9-min.pdf

7. https://www.researchgate.net/publication/340815293_Forced_Marriage

8. https://theexodusroad.com/forced-marriage-and-human-trafficking/

CHAPTER TWO

MULTIDISCIPLINARY EDUCATION: THE MASTER KEY OF NEP 2020 FOR QUALITY TRANSFORMATION IN HIGHER EDUCATION

Dr. V. V. Patil

Associate Professor,

Dr. M. H. A. College of Education,

Malegaon (Nashik)

ABSTRACT

India has a long tradition of holistic and multidisciplinary learning, from universities such as Takshashila and Nalanda, to the extensive literatures of India combining subjects across fields. Ancient Indian literary works such as Banabhatta's Kadambari described a good education as knowledge of the 64 Kalaas or arts; and among these 64 'arts' were not only subjects, such as singing and painting, but also 'scientific 'fields, such as chemistry and mathematics, 'vocational ' fields such as carpentry and clothes-making, 'professional 'fields, such as medicine and engineering, as well as 'soft skills' such as communication, discussion, and debate.

The very idea that all branches of creative human endeavour, including mathematics, science, vocational subjects, professional subjects, and soft skills should be considered 'arts', has distinctly Indian origins. This notion of a 'knowledge of many arts' or what in modern times is often called the 'liberal arts' (i.e., a liberal notion of the arts) must be brought back to Indian education, as it is exactly the kind of education that will be required for the 21st century. Assessments of educational approaches in undergraduate education that integrate the humanities and arts with Science, Technology, Engineering and Mathematics (STEM) have consistently showed positive learning outcomes, including increased creativity and innovation, critical thinking and higher-order thinking capacities, problem-solving abilities, teamwork, communication skills, more in-depth learning and mastery of curricula across fields, increases in social and moral awareness, etc., besides general engagement and enjoyment of learning. Research is also improved and enhanced through a holistic and multidisciplinary education approach.

Keywords: Multidisciplinary Education, NEP 2020, Quality Transformation, Higher Education

INTRODUCTION

A holistic and multidisciplinary education would aim to develop all capacities of human beings -intellectual, aesthetic, social, physical, emotional, and moral in an integrated manner. Such an education will help develop well-rounded individuals that possess critical 21st century capacities in fields across the arts, humanities, languages, sciences, social sciences, and professional, technical, and vocational fields; an ethic of social engagement; soft skills, such as communication, discussion and debate; and rigorous specialization in a chosen field or fields. Such a holistic education shall be, in the long term, the approach of all undergraduate programmes, including those in professional, technical, and vocational disciplines.

A HOLISTIC AND MULTIDISCIPLINARY EDUCATION

A holistic and multidisciplinary education, as described so beautifully in India's past, is indeed what is needed for the education of India to lead the country into the 21st century and the fourth industrial revolution. Even engineering institutions, such as IITs, will move towards more holistic and multidisciplinary education with more arts and humanities. Students of arts and humanities will aim to learn more science and all will make an effort to incorporate more vocational subjects and soft skills.

Institutional Restructuring and Consolidation

The main thrust of this policy regarding higher education is to end the fragmentation of higher education by transforming higher education institutions into large multidisciplinary universities, colleges, and HEI clusters/Knowledge Hubs, each of which will aim to have 3,000 or more students. This would help build vibrant communities of scholars and peers, break down harmful silos, enable students to become well-rounded across disciplines including artistic, creative, and analytic subjects as well as sports, develop active research communities across disciplines including cross-disciplinary research, and increase resource efficiency, both material and human, across higher education.

Multidisciplinary Universities

Moving to large multidisciplinary universities and HEI clusters is thus the highest recommendation of this policy regarding the structure of higher education. The ancient Indian universities Takshashila, Nalanda, Vallabhi, and Vikramshila, which had thousands of students from India and the world studying in vibrant multidisciplinary environments, amply demonstrated the type of great success that large multidisciplinary research and teaching universities could bring. India urgently needs to bring back this great Indian tradition to create well-rounded and innovative individuals, and which is already transforming other countries educationally and economically.

This vision of higher education will require, in particular, a new conceptual perception/understanding for what constitutes a higher education institution (HEI), i.e., a university or a college. A university will mean a multidisciplinary institution of higher learning that offers undergraduate and graduate programmes, with high quality teaching, research, and community engagement. The definition of university will thus allow a spectrum of institutions that range from those that place equal emphasis on teaching and research i.e., Research-intensive Universities, those that place greater emphasis on teaching but still conduct significant research i.e. Teaching-intensive Universities. Meanwhile, an Autonomous degree-granting College (AC) will refer to a large multidisciplinary institution of higher learning that grants undergraduate degrees and is primarily focused on undergraduate teaching though it would not be restricted to that and it need not be restricted to that and it would generally be smaller than a typical university.

A stage-wise mechanism for granting graded autonomy

A stage-wise mechanism for granting graded autonomy to colleges, through a transparent system of graded accreditation, will be established. Colleges will be encouraged, mentored, supported, and incentivized to gradually attain the minimum benchmarks required for each level of accreditation. Over a period of time, it is envisaged that every college would develop into either an

Autonomous degree-granting College, or a constituent college of a university - in the latter case, it would be fully a part of the university. With appropriate accreditations, Autonomous degree-granting Colleges could evolve into Research-intensive or Teaching-intensive Universities, if they so aspire.

It must be clearly stated that these three broad types of institutions are not in any natural way a rigid, exclusionary categorization, but are along a continuum. HEIs will have the autonomy and freedom to move gradually from one category to another, based on their plans, actions, and effectiveness. The most salient marker for these categories of institutions will be the focus of their goals and work. The Accreditation System will develop and use appropriately different and relevant norms across this range of HEIs. However, the expectations of high quality of education, and of teaching-learning, across all HEIs will be the same.

In addition to teaching and research, HEIs will have other crucial responsibilities, which they will discharge through appropriate resourcing, incentives, and structures. These include supporting other HEIs in their development, community engagement and service, contribution to various fields of practice, faculty development for the higher education system, and support to school education.

By 2040, all higher education institutions (HEIs) shall aim to become multidisciplinary institutions and shall aim to have larger student enrolments preferably in the thousands, for optimal use of infrastructure and resources, and for the creation of vibrant multidisciplinary communities. Since this process will take time, all HEIs will firstly plan to become multidisciplinary by 2030, and then gradually increase student strength to the desired levels.

Multidisciplinary Education policy in public and private institutions

Growth will be in both public and private institutions, with a strong emphasis on developing a large number of outstanding public institutions. There will be a fair and transparent system for determining increased levels of public funding support for public HEIs. This system will give an equitable opportunity for all public institutions to grow and develop, and will be based on transparent, pre-announced criteria from within the accreditation norms of the Accreditation System. HEIs delivering education of the highest quality as laid down in this Policy will be incentivized in expanding their capacity.

Institutions will have the option to run Open Distance Learning (ODL) and online programmes, provided they are accredited to do so, in order to enhance their offerings, improve access, increase GER, and provide opportunities for lifelong learning (SDG 4). All ODL programmes and their components leading to any diploma or degree will be of standards and quality equivalent to the highest quality programmes run by the HEIs on their campuses. Top institutions accredited for ODL will be encouraged and supported to develop high-quality online courses. Such quality online courses will be suitably integrated into curricula of HEIs, and blended mode will be preferred.

TOWARDS A MORE HOLISTIC AND MULTIDISCIPLINARY EDUCATION

The new regulatory system envisioned by this Policy will foster this overall culture of empowerment and autonomy to innovate, including by gradually phasing out the system of 'affiliated colleges' over a period of fifteen years through a system of graded autonomy, and to be carried out in a challenge mode. Each existing affiliating university will be responsible for mentoring its affiliated colleges so that they can develop their capabilities and achieve minimum benchmarks in academic and curricular matters; teaching and assessment; governance reforms; financial robustness; and administrative efficiency. All colleges currently affiliated to a university shall attain the required benchmarks over time to secure the prescribed accreditation benchmarks and eventually become autonomous degree-granting colleges. This will be achieved through a concerted national effort including suitable mentoring and governmental support for the same.

Imaginative and flexible curricular structures will enable creative combinations of disciplines for study, and would offer multiple entry and exit points, thus, removing currently prevalent rigid boundaries and creating new possibilities for life-long learning. Graduate-level, masters and doctoral education in large multidisciplinary universities, while providing rigorous research-based specialization, would also provide opportunities for multidisciplinary work, including in academia, government, and industry.

Large multidisciplinary universities and colleges will facilitate the move towards high-quality holistic and multidisciplinary education. Flexibility in curriculum and novel and engaging course options will be on offer to students, in addition to rigorous specialization in a subject or subjects. This will be encouraged by increased faculty and institutional autonomy in setting curricula. Pedagogy will have an increased emphasis on communication, discussion, debate, research, and opportunities for cross-disciplinary and interdisciplinary thinking.

Departments in Languages, Literature, Music, Philosophy, Indology, Art, Dance, Theatre, Education, Mathematics, Statistics, Pure and Applied Sciences, Sociology, Economics, Sports, Translation and Interpretation, and other such subjects needed for a multidisciplinary, stimulating Indian education and environment will be established and strengthened at all HEIs. Credits will be given in all Bachelor's Degree programmes for these subjects if they are done from such departments or through ODL mode when they are not offered in-class at the HEI.

The structure and lengths of degree programmes shall be adjusted accordingly. The undergraduate degree will be of either 3 or 4-year duration, with multiple exit options within this period, with appropriate certifications, e.g., a certificate after completing 1 year in a discipline or field including vocational and professional areas, or a diploma after 2 years of study, or a Bachelor 's degree after a 3-year programme. The 4-year multidisciplinary Bachelor's programme, however, shall be the preferred option since it allows the opportunity to experience the full range of holistic and multidisciplinary education in addition to a focus on the chosen major and minors as per the choices of the student. An Academic Bank of Credit (ABC) shall be established which would digitally store the academic credits earned from various recognized HEIs so that the degrees from an HEI can be awarded taking into account credits earned. The 4-year programme may also lead to a degree 'with Research' if the student completes a rigorous research project in their major area(s) of study as specified by the HEI.

HEIs will have the flexibility to offer different designs of Master's programmes: (a) there may be a 2-year programme with the second year devoted entirely to research for those who have completed the 3-year Bachelor 's programme; (b) for students completing a 4-year Bachelor 's programme with Research, there could be a 1-year Master's programme; and (c) there may be an integrated 5-year Bachelor's/Master's programme. Undertaking a Ph.D. shall require either a Master's degree or a 4-year Bachelor's degree with Research. The M.Phil. programme shall be discontinued.

Conclusion

The overall higher education sector will aim to be an integrated higher education system, including professional and vocational education. This Policy and its approach will be equally applicable to all HEIs across all current streams, which would eventually merge into one coherent ecosystem of higher education. University, worldwide, means a multidisciplinary institution of higher learning that offers undergraduate, graduate, and Ph.D. programmes, and engages in high-quality teaching and research. The present complex nomenclature of HEIs in the country such as 'deemed to be university', 'affiliating university', 'affiliating technical university', 'unitary university' shall be replaced simply by 'university' on fulfilling the criteria as per norms. HEIs will focus on research and innovation by setting up start-up incubation centres; technology development centres; centres in frontier areas of research; greater industry-academic linkages; and interdisciplinary research including humanities and social sciences research. Given the scenario of epidemics and pandemics, it is critical that HEIs take the lead to undertake research in areas of infectious diseases, epidemiology, virology, diagnostics, instrumentation, vaccinology and other relevant areas. HEIs will develop specific hand holding mechanisms and competitions for promoting innovation among student communities. The NRF will function to help enable and support such a vibrant research and innovation culture across HEIs, research labs, and other research organizations.

REFERENCE

1. "New Education Policy: There will be major changes in studies, exams, report cards". Till today. Retrieved 30 July 2020.
2. "BJP President JP Nadda said on the new education policy - The new education policy takes into account the needs of the new India". Punjab Kesari. 29 July 2020. Retrieved 30 July 2020.
3. New Education Policy, 2020
4. "New Education Policy-2020: Key Points at a Glance". 30 July 2020. Retrieved 30 July 2020.
5. "Let us know why a new National Education Policy was needed to change the education system of the country". Dainik Jagran. Retrieved 30 July 2020.
6. "New Education Policy 2020: Study till 5th now in mother tongue, a test for admission till graduation". Amar Ujala. Retrieved 31 July 2020.
7. "New Education Policy". Navbharat Times. Retrieved 31 July 2020.
8. "New Education Policy: There will be major changes in studies, exams, report cards". Till today. Retrieved 30 July 2020.
9. "New Education Policy 2020: Major changes in school

education, board exam, graduation degree, know 20 special things". Hindustan Live. Retrieved 30 July 2020. [dead links]

10. Singh, Professor Dinesh (29 July 2020). "New education policy will open the shackles of school and higher education". The Quint. Retrieved 30 July 2020.

11. "New Education Policy: Now students will be able to study music with chemistry, fashion designing with physics". Till today. Retrieved 30 July 2020.

12. "How much will the education system change with the new education policy? Know what the experts say". Till today. Retrieved 31 July 2020.

13. "Supporting the new education policy, Shashi Tharoor said - Many targets beyond reality, concern over budget". Till today. Retrieved 31 July 2020.

14. Singh, Saroj (30 July 2020). "New Education Policy 2020: RSS's agenda only or common people's talk too". BBC Hindi. Retrieved 31 July 2020.

15. NEP 2020: Student, Teacher Bodies Call The New Education Policy 'Anti-democratic'

16. Rohatgi, Anubha, Ed. (2020-08-07). "Highlights | NEP will play role in reducing gap between research and education in India: PM Modi". Hindustan Times. Retrieved 2020-08-08.

CHAPTER THREE

PROBLEMATICS OF NATIONAL IDENTITY IN "THE SHADOW LINES" OF AMITAV GHOSH

Swati Dattatraya Patil

Ph.D. Research Scholar,

Department of English, SAGE University,

Indore

ABSTRACT

Freedom from political colonialism came as a refreshing wind to the Indian writers who were now enthused to write with new outlook and express their indigenous ethos and beliefs. Post-colonial Indian English writers like Salman Rushdie, Vikram Seth , Amitav Ghosh etc., writing with great dynamism, distinctive voice, vigor and a level of self-reliance, have liberated Indian English literature from the colonial yoke. Historical nationalist issues such as diaspora, migration, refugees, colonial hegemony; socio-economic and cultural issues like east-west encounter, caste and class etc. become the concerns of these writers.

The present paper is intended to examine Amitav Ghosh" treatment of the problematic of identity in "The Shadow Lines" (1988), which as a memory novel, sketches few historical events like the freedom movement in Bengal, the Second World War and the Partition of India in 1947 and the communal riots in Bangladesh and

India. In this novel, Ghosh problematizes nationalism in his search for identity. The fervent nationalism upheld by grandmother is put to question and re-analysis. Ghosh explores the unreality and invalidity of traditional identity constructions such as nation and nationalism.

Keywords: Identity, Nationality, "The Shadow Lines", Trans-nationality, Individual Nationality

INTRODUCTION

Freedom from political colonialism came as a refreshing wind to the Indian writers who were now enthused to write with new outlook and express their indigenous ethos and beliefs. Post-colonial Indian English writers like Salman Rushdie, Vikram Seth, Amitav Ghosh etc, writing with great dynamism, distinctive voice, vigor and a level of self-reliance, have liberated Indian English literature from the colonial yoke. Historical nationalist issues such as diaspora, migration, refugees, colonial hegemony; socio-economic and cultural issues like east-west encounter, caste and class etc. become the concerns of these writers. The present paper is intended to examine Amitav Ghosh's treatment of the problematic of identity in "The Shadow Lines" (1988), which as a memory novel, sketches few historical events like the freedom movement in Bengal, the Second World War and the Partition of India in 1947 and the communal riots in Bangladesh and India.

TRAUMA OF PARTITION RIOTS

A highly innovative, complex and celebrated novel of Amitav Ghosh, "The Shadow Lines" Presents the trauma of partition riots. "Ghosh has edged up his novel to confront the memory of traumatic events." What implies the partition is not linear as Ghosh's novel which is written in the non- linear mode – an aspect which implies its title also -the shadowiness of the border line. But this border line – as an abstract construction - contributes only to problematize the situations and relations of a large number of people across it. Keeping this aspect in mind, this paper is prepared as a critique of Ghosh's treatment of the problematic of national identity. The novel depicts a wide, cosmopolitan scenario- most of the major events take place either in London or Dhaka and the protagonist, at present, lives with his family in Calcutta. "The novel superbly demonstrates the arrival of modernism in India."

Partition of people and that way, the issue of national identity need to be viewed from two angles – political and social – cultural or psychological. Issues like identity within a constructed national identity and feeling of oneness/ nationality crossing one's political territory are central to the discussion of the problematic of national identity in "The Shadow Lines". To conceptualize these aspects, it seems necessary that we clarify the idea of identity and in – between spaces in Ghosh. Standing as a unique creative writer in English following Rushdie, Amitav Ghosh deals with effects of colonialism. His writings while resisting generic divisions problematize the dominant discourse of history. One of the persistent idea in Ghosh's writing is the „in – between" Space. It is evident that Ghosh contests the contractedness of various borders separating one nation / race / culture from the others. In his quest for identity, Ghosh (i) revises his approach to history; (ii) destabilizes the borders and (iii) Scrutinizes the suppressed voices.

PROBLEMATICS OF INDIVIDUAL IDENTITY

Identity is a very debatable proposition/ question, both

theoretically and practically. The theoretical debate about identity concerns its nature, process of formation and its existential questions. Whereas essentialists believe in singularity of individual's identity, the post – modernists deny any such identity. Identity construction has been thus debated time and again, but one must acknowledge that an individual's identity is to as large extent formed by his / her social location which include his/her race, class, gender, etc. These problematics of individual identity have been applied / noticed in the national context in Ghosh's novel" The Shadow Lines" – the title itself suggesting the unreality and invalidity of constructions such as nation and nationality . The Shadowiness of the border line puts a question mark to the geographic boundary line between countries / nations and thus its identity. Ghosh considers space / place as non-neutral, non-objective. To him „a place does not merely exist. It has to be invented in one's imaginations. Ghosh presents it through Tridib's concept of space which was vast and comprehensive. Tridib"s mind strove to a place where there was no border between oneself and one"s image in the mirror.

PROBLEMATICS OF NATIONAL IDENTITY

Ghosh problematizes nationalism in his search for identity". "The Shadow Lines" interrogates national division backed by political consciousness and underlines the idea of emergence of a new world situation being hatched by the capitalist world economy. With the trans-nationalization of the forces of production and spread of market, the familiar national boundaries are pushed back to the darkness or the shadow. In this novel „a world beyond nation" has been posited as an ideal form of existence. This is most desirable in view of the growth of international capitalism and global market which demand freedom from the obstruction of national boundaries. "The Shadows Lines" interrogates the process through which a sense of national identity is constructed.

The construction of national identity is said to be the result of a dual dynamics one homogenizing and the other differentiating. Construction of the idea of a nation or community as homogenous, i.e. unified & single, also suggests its difference from other nations or communities. Thus being Indian means being members of a single unified family sharing common goals and aspirations. This very concept of Indian will differentiate him / her from a Pakistani, an American or a British. Ghosh, striking at this very core of the dynamics of nationhood, shows that the idea of a nation is a misleading construction. One fundamental question the novel raises is –"Is the nation a homogeneous entity?" which is univocally answered with a firm and emphatic "No". The incidents that inspired Ghosh to write the novel - inhuman massacre of the Sikhs following assassination of Indira Gandhi by the non-Sikh countrymen who deeply pained Ghosh- is a proof that the claim of a homogenized nation is baseless. Though the riots erupting in the aftermath of Indira's assassination are not mentioned in the novel, there are a number of Incidents to prove that the nation of India as a homogenous community was shattered for Ghosh.

Communal riots consequent to defilement of Hazratbal Shrine in 1964 is a fitting example. The narrator of "The Shadow Lines" as a school boy remembers how ill-feelings & suspicions poisoned the harmonious life of the Hindus & the Muslims. Rumours were that one community had poisoned the water supply to exterminate the other community. The whole atmosphere was filled with suspicions, fear and hatred. Through the narrator's growth from childhood to adulthood, Ghosh has shown that the idea of a national border is just a mirage. The deceptive nature of the national borders that are constructed to project an image of difference across political division is revealed in the novel. The narrator's grandmother firmly believes in the ability of national borders to differentiate her own community from other communities.

Her nationalistic beliefs seem to be undermined as the novel unfolds. In 1964 when she plans to visit Dhaka, she wonders whether she would be able to see the borders between India and East Pakistan from the air. When her grandson (the narrator) mocks her asking - if the border line was a long black line, she says, "of course not. But surely there's something – trenches perhaps, or soldiers or guns pointing at each other or even just barren strip of land. Don't they call it no-man's land?" with her experience of the traumatic events of the partition, grandmother's expectation of a border line is natural to her though absurd to others/us. With the unfolding of the novel, the grandmother is forced to realize the fact that the two sides of the border were merely the mirror image of each other .This realization in a sense pains her and forces her to interrogate the very purpose of the nationalist movement and the reasons of war between the nations. She tries to assert the necessity of a real demarcation. What were it all for then – Partition and all the killing and everything – if there isn't something in between?

SHADOWINESS OF IDENTITY CONSTRUCTION

The novelist brings out the arbitrary nature of the partition logic – that is, partition of India & Pakistan (Bangladesh) is illogical and arbitrary. The border lines are none but the arbitrary product of the politicians" whims. These arbitrary lines cannot really determine the cultural difference between the two communities living across the border. To quote Jethamosai, "I don't believe in this India – Shindia. It's all very well, you're going away now, but suppose when you set there they decide to draw another line somewhere? What will you do then? Where will you move to? No one will ever have you anywhere." The Shadowiness of the border line, and that way, the implication of the title of the novel, thus clearly stands stated.

Political division is arbitrary as it is arbitrarily taken and as such identity of the people across the so – called national border lines are imbalanced all the time. Notably this temporality of individual identity also suggests the temporality of the nation/national identity. The situation is succinctly brought out by Sadat Hassan Manto in the short story "Toba Tek Singh", where the so –called lunatic only presents sanity. To say, political division of nation(s) is nothing but a farcical act. "The partition of the country is rojected in the novel as an act of meaningless violence" In the novel there is a growing sense that the logic of the nation state is necessarily at odds with various forms of sub continental community – that to be Indian is to be perversely and perhaps unsuccessfully defined oneself against one"s mirror image from across the border.

Ghosh has shown in the novel that riots and distances at the social and national level do not really beget any solution through partition of the bigger nation – state. He has shown that violence does not get driven to the borders. Dhaka and Calcutta - the two different cities in two independent states - do not drift apart and become the other reality as they flare up at the slightest pretext. The pattern of violence in these cities relates them to each other. The narrator undertakes a voyage into this land which exists outside space, an expense without distances and a land of looking glass events. He is simply amazed to discover that the border could not separate these places, rather locked them into irreversible symmetry. He witnessed identical scenes of violence on both sides, with few human incidents of saving lives - indicative of indivisible sanity that binds people to each other independent of their governments. The border line becomes just "a looking glass border". Ghosh acknowledges no separate national or cultural realities because for him all such demarcations are shadow lines, arbitrary and invented divisions. "The author boldly tackles political themes both national and international."

CONCLUSION

Ghosh in this way problematizes the idea of national identity. Interrogating Grandmother's fervent nationalism, Ghosh explores the unreality and invalidity of traditional identity constructions such as nation, nationality and nationalism. This he has brought to the forefront through three aspects : (1). Political borders are questioned and shown to be arbitrary – as they are whimsically taken by politicians, (2.) The idea of nationality – nation as a homogenous whole – has been contrasted – with inhumane activities poisoning the fraternal relationship among different races of the country and (3). The looking glass border has been set up – showing identical scenes of violence across border on the one hand and feeling of oneness with people of other countries on the other. Ghosh in "The Shadow Lines" attempts to create the image of the global umbrella which includes and encompasses various cultures and create a single unified global picture.

REFERENCES

1. Manjula Saxena, The Shadow Lines as a Memory Novel, in Arvind Chowdhary (Ed) Amitav Ghosh"s The Shadow Lines- Critical Essays (New Delhi: Atlantic publishers & distributors(p) Ltd, 2008) 39. („Ghosh has made maximum and effective use of memory in almost all its dimensions and forms"-Saxena writes)

2. Murari Prasad, The Shadow Lines –A quest for indivisible sanity, in Mithilesh k. Pandey (Ed) Contemporary Indian literature in English- A humanistic perspective. (New Delhi: Kalyani Publishers,1999) 56.

3. Rangrao Bhongle, The Evils of cosmopolitanism: a native approach to Amitav Ghosh"s The shadow Lines, in Rangrao Bhognle (Ed) The inside view – Native responses to contemporary Indian English Novel. (New Delhi: Atlantic Publishers & Distributors (P) Ltd, 2003) 131.

4. Amitav Ghosh, The Shadow Lines, (Ravi Dayal Publisher & Penguin Books, 2009) 23 (All subsequent textual references presented within brackets are to this edition)

5. Sukanta Das, Beyond the frontiers: Quest for identity in Amitav Ghosh"s The Shadow Lines, in The Atlantic Critical Review Quarterly. Vol-8 No-1, Jan – March, 2009, 87.

6. Amitav Ghosh, "The Ghost of Mrs. Gandhi" in New Yorker, 17 July 1995. (Ghosh states that he got inspiration to write "The Shadow Lines" from the anti Sikh riots of 1984 in Delhi. "It became a book not about anyone event but about the meaning of such events through them", he writes).

7. Someswar Sati – Interrogating the nation, Growing global in

The Shadow Lines in Arvind Chowdhary (Ed) Amitav Ghosh"s The Shadow Lines- Critical Essays (New Delhi: Atlantic publishers & distributors(p) Ltd, 2008) 56.

CHAPTER FOUR

FLIPPED CLASSROOM: A NEW APPROACH IN THE FIELD OF TEACHING AND LEARNING

Smt. Saba Hassan

Assistant Professor,

Islamia College of Education,

Hyderabad

CONCEPT AND MEANING OF FLIPPED CLASSROOM

A flipped classroom is an instructional strategy and a type of blended learning that reverses the traditional learning environment by delivering instructional content, often online, outside of the classroom. It moves activities, including those that mayhave been traditionally considered homework, into the classroom. In a flipped classroom, students watch online lectures, collaborate in online discussions, or carry out research at home while engaging in concepts in the classroom with the guidance of a mentor.

In the traditional model of classroom instruction, the teacher is typically the central focus of a lesson and the primary disseminator of information during the class period. The teacher responds to questions while students defer directly to the teacher for guidance and feedback. In a classroom with a traditional style of instruction, individual lessons may be focused on an explanation of content utilizing a lecture-style. Student engagement in the traditional model may be limited to activities in which students work independently or in small groups on an application task designed by the teacher. Class discussions are typically centred on the teacher, who controls the flow of the conversation. Typically, this pattern of teaching also involves giving students the task of reading from a textbook or practicing a concept by working on a problem set, for example, outside school.

The flipped classroom intentionally shifts instruction to a learner-centered model in which class time explores topics in greater depth and creates meaningful learning opportunities, while <u>educational technologies</u> such as online videos are used to 'deliver content' outside of the classroom. In a flipped classroom, 'content delivery' may take a variety of forms. Often, video lessons prepared by the teacher or third parties are used to deliver content, although online collaborative discussions, digital research, and text readings may be used. It has been shown that the ideal length of the video lesson to be is eight to twelve minutes.

Flipped classrooms also redefine in-class activities. In-class lessons accompanying flipped classroom may include activity learning or more traditional homework problems, among other practices, to engage students in the content.

A teacher's interaction with students in a flipped classroom can be more personalized and less didactic, and students are actively involved in knowledge acquisition and construction as they participate in and evaluate their learning.

The Definition of Flipped Classroom

A flipped classroom is one where students have introduced to content at home, and practice working through it at school.

In this blended learning approach, face-to-face interactions are mixed with independent study via technology. Students watch pre-recorded videos at home, and then come to school to do the homework armed with questions and at least some background knowledge.

The concept behind the flipped classroom is rethinking when students have access to the resources they need most. If the problem is that students need help doing the work rather than being introduced to the new thinking behind the work, than the solution the flipped classroom takes is to reverse that pattern.

This doubles student access to teachers–once with the videos at home, and again in the classroom, increasing the opportunity for personalization and more precise guiding of learning. In the flipped classroom model, students practice under the guidance of the teacher, while accessing content on their own.

A side benefit is that teachers can record lectures that emphasize critical ideas, power standards, and even the pace of a given curriculum map. It also has the side benefit of allowing students to pause, rewind, and Googleterms;rematch, etc., as well as creating a ready-made library for student review, make-up work, etc.

IMPORTANCE/CHARACTERISTICS OF FLIPPED CLASSROOM

There are various benefits attributed to the idea of utilizing the Flipped Classroom approach, some including:

1. A college reading empirical study identifies Flipped Classroom's approach at including all forms of learning (i.e. oral, visual, listening, hands on, problem solving, etc.).

2. Rather than learning in a traditional classroom setting, Flipped

Classroom uses a more application-based approach for students (i.e. hands on and problem solving activities).

3. The accessibility of Flipped Classroom is extremely convenient, especially for students that would face difficulties in traveling to the physical classroom. Such students would still have the foundational information of the course at hand via online.

4. Communication is greatly emphasized in a Flipped Classroom setting, essentially referring to: student-student and student-teacher interactions.

5. Flipped Classroom utilizes a student-centered teaching modelled in order to ensure that the course is primarily aimed at contributing to the student's overall success in obtaining a proper, effective education.

6. Essentially avoids the overarching idea of "cramming" for exams and forgetting the information post-examination, as it encourages students to understand the underlying rationale behind the information provided being provided to them.

7. Students must account for the responsibilities given to them in regards to learning the foundational information provided, as their personal work and contribution will be reflected in the grade that they receive at the end of the course. This will, in turn, make them better prepared for future, more difficult courses.

OTHER EDUCATIONAL APPROACHES WITH FLIPPED CLASSROOM

1. Flipped learning + Peer instruction

Interactive method based on collaborative work that has proven effective in areas such as science, technology, engineering and mathematics (Dumont, 2014). Specifically consists of sharing with other students a different response to their own and explain the reasons that support the same to learn from each other. In this process, the reasoning beyond the answers is analysed.

2. Flipped mastery learning

When the invested learning model is applied in a more advanced way. Educators begin by organizing content around specific goals. Students work on course content at their own pace and upon reaching the end of each unit, they must show mastery of learning objectives before moving on to the next topic and so on. Students can show evidence of their learning through videos, worksheets, experimental stories, programs, projects, examples, among others. There are two challenges in the flipped-mastery model: the first is to deliver instruction to students when they have different levels of learning and understanding of the subjects. The second challenge is to carry out summative assessment when the student has to be evaluated more than once.

3. Flipped adaptive learning

The combination of inverted learning and other pedagogical approaches such as <u>adaptive learning</u> can help educators obtain information from the areas of learning that dominate their students and those in which they still have deficiencies or need to improve. This knowledge can support the teacher in determining how to organize and manage class time in order to maximize student learning.

4. Flipped learning + Gamification

A step forward in the flipped-mastery model would be to

include <u>gamification</u> elements in the learning process. Gamification is the application of game mechanisms in situations not directly related to games. The basic idea is to identify what motivates a game and see how it can be applied in the teaching-learning model (in this case it would be Flipped-Mastery). The results of the Fun Theory research showed that fun could significantly change people's behaviour in a positive sense, in the same way that it has a positive effect on education.

5. Flipped learning + cooperative learning

There may also be a symbiosis or complementation between the flipped classroom technique and <u>cooperative learning</u>. Schoolwork, also commonly known as "homework", is done jointly and in cooperation with the group as the teacher moves the time spent explaining the subject to the flipped classroom method. In this way, the student has to assimilate and understand the content of more theoretical weight at home, through the recordings made by the teacher, and the time in class is dedicated to the development of tasks and problem solving and doubts through cooperative learning.

6. Flipped learning + Inclusive classroom

The qualities of a flipped classroom that are valuable for typical students can also benefit students with disabilities. Inclusive classrooms can be used to change perceptions and reduce the stigma students with disabilities experience.For example, a teacher can develop a lesson about social skills if it is an area of concern for a student diagnosed with Autism Spectrum Disorder.

ADVANTAGES OF FLIPPED CLASSROOM

1. Dive deeper into subject -When students have a basic knowledge about a certain subject, you can dive deeper into the

learning material. You can offer more learning material to students who are looking for a challenge.

2. Lectures can be reused -It can take a lot of time to prepare homework for students. But once you got it all, it's easy to re-use your lectures for next year.

3. Transparency for parents -It gives parents the chance to take a look into their children's video lectures. Once children don't understand a certain concept, parents are able to help them.

4. Students have more control - In a flipped classroom, it is possible for students to have increased input and control over their own learning. By providing short lectures at home, students are given the freedom to learn at their own pace. Students may pause or rewind the lectures, write down questions they may have, and discuss them with their teachers and peers in class. This also allows students who need more time to understand certain concepts to take their time reviewing the material without getting left behind, and receives immediate assistance from teachers and classmates. As a result, this can not only improves student achievement, but improves student behaviour in class as well.

5. It promotes student-centered learning and collaboration - The project-based work that now takes place in the classroom need not be on an individual basis. A flipped classroom enables students to spend more time collaborating with one another: not only a great way to learn, but also good for their team working skills. Flipped classrooms allows class time be used to master skills through collaborative projects and discussions. This encourages students to teach and learn concepts from each other with the guidance of their teachers. By allowing students to partake in their own learning, they are able to own the knowledge they achieve, which in turn builds confidence. Furthermore, teachers are given the ability to identify errors in thinking or concept application, and are more available for one-on-one interaction.

6. Lessons and content are more accessible (provided there is tech access) - By making video lectures available at all times online, students who are forced to miss class due to illness, sports, vacations or emergencies, can catch up quickly. This also gives teachers more flexibility when they themselves are sick and eliminates make-up assignments.

7. Access=easier for parents to see what's going on - Unlike traditional classroom models, flipped classrooms give parents 24/7 access to their student's video lectures. This allows parents to be better prepared when attempting to help their students and gives them insight into the quality of instruction their students are receiving.

8. It can be more efficient - Done properly, in a flipped classroom; kids can have more time to be kids, whether that means more free time, or practice that is more academic.

9. More one-to-one time between teacher and student - A flipped classroom dramatically increases the amount of time you have to spend with each student. It also create a platform for them to ask questions or seek extra help with an area they're finding challenging.

10. Students learn at their own pace - Because 'knowledge acquisition' now takes place outside the classroom, each student can control it to match their own personal abilities and appetite. A traditional classroom instruction-based method relies on every student absorbing and understanding at the same time and pace. Flipped learning does not. This can be particularly liberating for slower learners. No longer, do they feel the burden of having to 'keep up'; they are free to learn in a way that works for them. In addition, if they want to go back and study something again, they can.When students prepare their class, they can work whenever they want and take whatever time it takes to finish (as long as it is before the deadline).

11. It encourages students to come to class prepared - Students can follow courses where teachers put on homework students have to prepare. Teachers are able to track the progress of students and view their results. This makes it possible to have a clear idea of what the struggles are of your students and see what students struggle the most. Furthermore, it allows teacher to identify errors in thinking or concept application.After students have engaged with digital content at home, they can come to the classroom prepared with ideas and questions. It's a great way to involve students in shaping the classroom sessions, and thereby nurture their sense of responsibility.

12. Practical things – like missing class due to illness – become less problematic - It used to be that, if a student missed a lesson, they missed learning something. Not with flipped learning. Because students engage with a lesson on their own time, and away from school, absence need not detract from them learning the material.

13. Subject matter content becomes infinitely richer - Previously, students were only exposed to one source of information on a topic: that which the teacher gave them in class. With flipped learning, they can explore much more. They can access multiple sources, and equally you can direct them towards sources from other teachers, and more. This diversity will only increase their comprehension of the subject.

14.Its cost-effective - Because students use their own devices to access content, there's no need for a school to invest in hundreds of new computers or classroom gadgets. The only thing you now need to give: more of your personal time and attention

DISADVANTAGES OF FLIPPED CLASSROOM

1. It can create or exacerbate a digital divide - One of the most prominent issues is the necessity for students to have access to a computer and Internet in order to view the lectures. This is particularly hard on students from low-income districts who already have limited access to resources.

2. Overly reliant on student trust - When you flip your classroom, you tend to delegate a lot of responsibility to learners. You rely on them to be diligent about, for instance, watching prescribed videos or reviewing important materials before each face-to-face interaction. In some flipped classroom examples, like mandatory **compliance training**, such over-reliance might not be appropriate or safe.

3. Networking opportunities restricted - The disadvantages of flipped classroom courses also include diminished opportunities for staff from dispersed areas of the company to meet more frequently to network. By limiting in-person meet ups to a select number of occasions, flipped classroom learning potentially prevents future colleagues, peers, and supervisors from getting together to know each other and establish connections that can be leveraged in the future.

4. Denies learners "face time" - Since this approach relies heavily on flipped classroom tools like video-on-demand, pre-recorded voice lectures, and archived learning **content**, learners aren't offered the same amount of access and face time to lecturers as they would receive in traditional learning.

5. Technology issues - No access to internet means no homework. Once students do not make their homework, other things easily distract them. In addition, you don't want that to happen. Nowadays, there are a lot less technology options. So, this issue will become less and less relevant.

6. Organization -The first time you implement the flipped classroom; it will have to be a lot of organization. Teachers have to introduce the students to the completely different concept. This can take some time, because they go from a more passive learning style to an active learning style.

7. Lack of motivation -You always have to be motivated to do your homework and be prepared for class. If you do not, other things' easily distract you. When you don't have the basic knowledge, its hard dive deeper into a subject. Teachers should really motivate students to do their homework;otherwise,there is no flipped classroom.

8. Not for every student -"Meta cognitive skills" seems like a difficult word, but is easy to explain. It's about knowing how to learn and on what learning style suits you best. The flipped classroom requires a lot of self-discipline. Students have to know how to learn, this will come with time.

BENEFITS OF FLIPPED CLASSROOM FOR STUDENTS

The classical setting of a classroom is all about the teacher and the teacher's needs. All the tools are the teacher has to use, for the best delivery of instruction. The students are merely passive receivers of information.However, whoever entered a classroom knows that students are anything but passive. Their natural curiosity makes them actively seek new knowledge, and when they are passionate about a subject they try to learn all there is to be learned about it. A student-cantered approach to teaching shifts the focus from the teacher's needs to the students. In addition, this is what the flipped classroom model supports:

1. When students watch or listen to lectures at home, and then solve problems and apply the new knowledge in the classroom, they get less frustration with their homework.

2. When they do not understand a new concept, they can ask questions and get immediate targeted answers.

3. The time spent in the classroom becomes not enough for all the conversations and collaboration that inevitably spur from exploring subjects in a deeper manner.

4. Finally yet importantly, students who are absent due to illness, too long a commute, or any other reason, can catch up with their peers faster and easier with the flipped classroom model than with the standard one.

BENEFITS OF FLIPPED CLASSROOM FOR TEACHERS

With a ton of information available at the fingertips of whoever cares to search for it, teachers are no longer the only source of knowledge for students. However,don't get me wrong; they aren't obsolete either. In fact, they are more important than ever.

A flipped classroom is more demanding than the traditional one. Teachers need to identify the individual learning needs of students, making sure they all use the class time engaged with the learning process. Moreover, this can be harder than the traditional teaching model. At the same time, it comes with a set of rewards:

1. When students come prepared to class, there is little to no need for teachers to address content related questions. Instead, they can support students in better understanding the concepts through practical application.

2. Once a lecture had done, it can be reused as many times as the teacher wants, until the content becomes out-dated. However, H_2O will always be the symbol of water, the same as Alaska will always be the biggest US state in terms of area.

3. The flipped classroom gives more freedom to teachers to decide upon how much time to spend with each student. Struggling students, great performers, introverted kids, and extroverted ones can get the attention each of them needs.

4. Finally yet importantly, it offers more transparency for parents, who will know exactly what their kids are preparing for at school. This can also improve the communication between parents and teachers.

The flipped classroom inspires teachers to offer a versatile and engaging way to share learning content, while putting more control into students' hands regarding their own learning processes.

CHAPTER FIVE

MIND MAPPING: A NEW TEACHING LEARNING STRATEGY

Jyoti Narayan Shrote

Assistant Professor,

Indira College of Commerce and Science,

Pune 33

CONCEPT AND MEANING OF MIND MAPPING

According to Johanna Brams, (MSEDT, Lehigh University) "Organizing ideas and concepts into graphic patterns has been explored for years by cognitive educators. Mind Mapping builds a process structure or "map" over the content body of the material a person has gathered, thereby organizing it for development. Constructivism, simply stated, is the philosophy that we learn by organizing new concepts and ideas relative to our own experience. Mind Mapping mirrors the constructivist theory. Research has shown that developing mind maps increases thinking, memory and learning skills. Recently Lehigh acquired a software program called Mind View, which takes the idea of Mind Mapping to a new level."

Amind map is a graphical way to represent ideas and concepts. It is a visual thinking tool that helps structuring information, helping you to better analyze, comprehend, synthesize, recall and generate new ideas.In a mind map, as opposed to traditional note taking or a linear text, information is structured in a way that resembles much more closely how your brain actually works. Since it is an activity that is both analytical and artistic, it engages your brain in a much, much richer way, helping in all its cognitive functions.

A mind map is an easy way to brainstorm thoughts organically without worrying about order and structure. It allows you to visually structure your ideas to help with analysis and recall.

A mind map is a diagram for representing tasks, words, concepts, or items linked to and arranged around a central concept or subject using a non-linear graphical layout that allows the user to build an intuitive framework around a central concept. A mind map can turn a long list of monotonous information into a colourful, memorable and highly organized diagram that works in line with your brain's natural way of doing things.

A mind map can be used as a simplified content management system (CMS). It allows you to store all your data in a centralized location to stay organized. With the various mind mapping software programs out today, you can attach files to different branches for even more flexibility. You can also change to various different views in order to find one that suits you best.

Graphical technique for visualizing connections between several ideas or pieces of information. Each idea or fact is written down and then linked by lines or curves to its major or minor (or following or previous) idea or fact, thus creating a web of relationships. Developed by the UK researcher Tony Buzan in his 1972 book 'Use Your Head,' mind mapping is used in note taking, brainstorming, problem solving, and project planning. Like other mapping techniques its purpose is to focus attention, and to capture and frame knowledge to facilitate sharing of ideas and concepts.

STRUCTURE OF MIND MAPPING

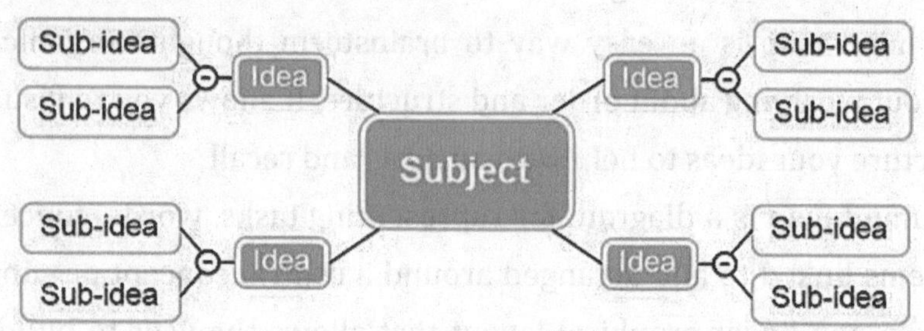

IMPORTANCE/NEED OF MIND MAPPING IN EDUCATION / TEACHING

1. Lesson Preparation - Teaching preparation can amount to files full of plans and documents, as a single lesson's preparation alone can generate reams of notes. By using Mind Mapping to plan your teaching, you can reduce the amount of notes you take into clear, concise plans which are easy to follow. With iMindMap, the Mind Mapping software tool, you can make organising teaching plans even easier, as you can access all of your notes, files and education website links from within one Mind Map.

2. Delivering Lessons - Mind Maps are ideal for teaching and presenting concepts in the classroom as they provide a useful focus for students, delivering an overview of the topic without superfluous information. Perfect for introducing a new subject in a way which is accessible and easy to follow, Mind Maps are an excellent way to present concepts and ideas. Now, with the advent of MindMap's award winning Presentation Mode, you can be sure to keep your students engaged and amazed as your branches smoothly animate to show your next point.

Curriculum Planning -Teaching today hinges around well-organised curriculum planning. With new curriculum initiatives, briefs, objectives and aims, it can all become overwhelming. But with Mind Mapping you can plan your year in sequence, prioritising key topics and adding deadlines as necessary. MindMap makes this process even more hassle-free through integration with Office software programmes, such as Microsoft Word and Excel. Plus, the MindMap Ultimate Project Management system gives you even more control over your annual plans, as you can add tasks, completion rates and deadlines to keep on top of your teaching schedule at all times.

4. Creating Handouts - Mind Maps are the ideal teaching tool for classroom handouts, as the inherent colour, images and visually appealing layout of a Mind Map engages students instantly. Mind Maps provide subject overviews succinctly, making even the most complex topic easy to understand and interesting. They are especially useful for visual learners, such as dyslexic students, who can feel frustrated and demotivated when being given information in linear, monochromatic format. With MindMap, teaching handouts can be shared in a number of digital formats (including image, PDF and web page) and printed in a variety of ways.

5. Encouraging Discussion and Independent Thought - The Cambridge Primary Review recently assessed that classroom interaction and listening to students was key for generating independent thought, a quality looked for by examiners and future employers. Mind Mapping is the perfect collaborative tool for class discussions, as the nature of the Mind Map encourages students to forge links between topics as well as forming their own ideas and opinions. With MindMap, this teaching process is made smoother than ever with Audio Notes to record class discussions as they happen and assign individual viewpoints to each branch.

6. Student Assessment - It is important to assess knowledge at the beginning of a topic and after to monitor your students understanding. Mind Mapping is a key tool for this concept, of preview and review/pre and post learning. Mind Maps encourages students to express ideas, from special needs and highly gifted students, and provides an accurate barometer of topic adoption.

7. Self-Evaluation - With frequent teacher inspections and reviews, it is important to constantly self-assess and evaluate your teaching style and preparation. Mind Mapping allows you to assess your current abilities (for example, in areas such as lesson delivery, handouts, interaction etc.) and then goal set what you would like to achieve within a week, a month, a year. This powerful form of self-evaluation will allow you to keep improving and meeting your teaching target objectives.

IMPLICATIONS OF MIND MAPPING IN CLASSROOM

The adoption of Mind Maps in teaching has grown recently due to the benefits of using Mind Maps to learn and the availability of free online mind mapping software.

Teachers have recognized the value of using Mind Maps to engage students, encourage creativity and, most importantly, teaching how to learn rather simply memorizing content. Mind Maps have even been integrated into emerging teaching techniques such as the Flipped Classroom and Design Thinking as outlined in the Mind Map on the right.

How do teachers harness the full power of Mind Mapping? Below are some ideas on how teachers and student can use Mind Maps both in and out of the classroom.

1. Planning - Whether its lesson plans, design of your class curriculum for the school year or planning an assignment timeline, Mind Maps give you a clear and visual overview of what needs to be covered.

2. Organizing - If you are the type of person who regularly jots down ideas and thoughts, Mind Maps are the perfect tool to create structure and organization of a topic.

3. Teaching - Online Mind Maps can be used in class to brainstorm and generate discussions. This will encourage students to participate but also to fully understand a topic and its nuances by creating connections between ideas.

4. Hand-outs -Mind Maps that have been created online can easily be printed and shared with students. Notes in the Mind Map can built on by students in class.

5. Presentations - A brilliant way to develop student's communication skills is through presentations. However, students can easily become bored listening to others present. Mind Maps act as visual information providers and encourage the audience to engage with the material that has being presented. Easily create an interactive Mind Map online with this free Mind Mapping tool, Exam Time.

6. Creativity - Essentially a Mind Map is a blank canvas; why not have some fun in your classroom? Get the creative juices flowing by throwing your students a silly idea and asking them how this can be achieved? Not only will this exercise encourage creativity, but it will also help students think for themselves and have some fun with it!

7. Learning - Mind Maps have been embraced in the realm of education as a learning tool which helps students reinforce knowledge by making connections between different areas and delving in-depth into an area.

8. Collaboration - The new generation of "Digital Citizens" are highly adaptable to change and expect to use technology as part of their education. Students can easily work together on group projects or assignments using free online study tools such as Exam Time where you can share your Mind Map with friends or a group of people.

9. Assessment - A great way to use Mind Maps for assessment is to ask students to express their ideas about a topic in a Mind Map before and after a class. Students will retain the information better and it will reassure teachers that students remember and understand the knowledge.

10. Comprehension -Analysing study material by reflecting on what you have learned is key to fully comprehending new information. Encourage students to delve into the material and see how far they can go – a Mind Map can develop into several ideas, which can branch out into new Mind Maps from each node.

ADVANTAGES/BENEFITS OF MIND MAPPING IN EDUCATION

1. Improved Memory & Recall -Mind maps are full of mental triggers that help your brain comprehend and store concepts more easily. You will take fewer notes, need fewer revisions and retain more facts than you would with linear notes!

2. Free Flow of Ideas - Because you mostly use keywords, images and short phrases in mind maps, you can jot down thoughts a lot faster than usual. This free flow of ideas will help you brainstorm creative writing assignments and solve brainteasers.

3. Structured Information -Mind maps can store and structure vast amounts of information. They display hierarchy, show relationships between single topics and enable you to see the "big picture" at a glance. This also makes them ideal for summarizing texts.

4. Better Communication -Cloud-based mind mapping helps foster collaboration between students and allows for a more efficient communication between teachers and students. Even the most complex problem has quickly visualized and explained with a map.

5. Wide Adaptability -Human brain works exactly the way how a mind map grows, thus allowing mind maps to be used in many occasions involving learning and arrangement, such as preparing an exam, taking notes, making a book summary, planning things and organizing structured tasks etc.

6. Convenient Editing -Comparing with traditional linear texts on notebooks, a mind map can theoretically develop into unlimited branches and levels in structure. It's easy and convenient to add ideas and information at any time later rather than squeezing texts into margins of the paper with messily distributed lines and arrows.

7. Enhance Memory - In addition to the radiant structure, the mapper can insert images and symbols to his map as he likes. These personalized elements are prone to make things easier to memorize.

8. Get People Focused - In the layout of a mind map, things delve from hyponym into hyponym. Such a structure help you focus on the links and relationships between ideas. In this case, you get comprehensive information instead of scattered facts.

Concise Information - Since the topic texts of mind maps are keywords and short phrases, a mind map is a great aid in condensing plenty of information. For example, when preparing the final exam, it is much more timesaving to review knowledge on a mind map than read the whole book.

DISADVANTAGES/LIMITATIONS OF MIND MAPPING IN EDUCATION

1. Texts Limitation -As has mentioned above, mind map topic texts consist of keywords and short phrases, which limit the quantity of texts you want to put in. On a hand-drawn mind map, large chunks of text will make the map look messy. However, if you choose to use mind map tool, you can insert notes, tags, comments, attachments and hyperlinks to add more information without displaying them.

2. Time-consuming - If you need to draw a delicate mind map with excellent pictures and accompanying texts, it may take some time. In this regard, making mind maps with outstanding mind map software such as Mind Master will save you energy and time.

3. Rules Limitation - Once you choose to draw mind maps with mind mapping software, you are not able to freestyle your map without limitations. The way software works follow certain rules, such as the layout, font, and theme are predefined. You are not allowed to develop the map as free as you can on paper.

CHAPTER SIX

CONCEPT MAPPING: GRAPHICAL INSTRUCTIVE WAY OF TEACHING AND LEARNING PROCESS

Manvita Shivdas Khairnar

Assistant Professor,

Vishwasattya College of Education,

Ojhar (Nashik)

CONCEPT AND MEANING OF CONCEPT MAPPING

Concept mapping is a structured process, focused on a topic or construct of interest, involving input from one or more participants, that produces an interpretable pictorial view (concept map) of their ideas and concepts and how these are interrelated.

Used as learning and teaching technique, concept mapping visually illustrates the relationships between concepts and ideas. Often represented in circles or boxes, concepts are linked by words and phrases that explain the connection between the ideas, helping students organize and structure their thoughts to further understand information and discover new relationships. Most concept maps represent a hierarchical structure, with the overall, broad concept first with connected sub-topics, more specific concepts

Concept mapping can be a powerful tool in the <u>world of education</u>, helping students to perform at higher cognitive levels and helping teachers to explain complicated subjects and assess student understanding.

A concept map is a type of <u>graphic organizer</u> used to help students organize and represent knowledge of a subject. Concept maps begin with a main idea (or concept) and then branch out to show how that main idea can be broken down into specific topics.

FEATURES OF CONCEPT MAPPING

Concept maps are also referred to as conceptual diagrams. While other types of diagrams may look similar, concept maps have specific characteristics differentiating them from other visual tools.

1. Concepts - Concepts are defined as "perceived regularities or patterns in events or objects, or records of events or objects, designated by a label" and are depicted as shapes in the diagram.

2. Linking words/phrases - Linking words or phrases are located on the lines connecting objects in a concept map, and these words describe the relationship between two concepts. They are as concise as possible and typically contain a verb. Examples include "causes," "includes" and "requires."

3. Propositional structure - Propositions are meaningful statements made up of two or more concepts connected with linking words. These statements are also known as semantic units or units of meaning. Concepts and propositions are the foundation for the creation of new knowledge in a domain. Essentially, a concept map visually conveys a set of propositions about a certain topic.

4. Hierarchical structure - A key element of the concept map is its hierarchical structure. The most general and inclusive concepts are positioned at the top of a concept map with the more specific and exclusive concepts arranged hierarchically below. As such, a concept map is designed to read from top to bottom.

5. Focus question - A focus question defines the issue or problem the concept map needs to solve. Developing a focus question allows you to design with a context in mind and thus helps guide and maintain the direction of your concept map. Within the hierarchical structure, the focus question should be at the very top of the concept map and serve as a reference point.

6. Parking lot - Before beginning your concept map, it can be helpful to come up with a list identifying the key concepts that need to be included. Establish a rank ordered list from the most general concept to the most specific. This list is referred to as a parking lot, as you will move the items into the map as you figure out where they fit in.

7. Cross-links - Cross-links are relationships between concepts in different domains of the concept map, allowing you to visualize how ideas within these different domains are connected. Both the cross-links and the hierarchical structure facilitate creative thinking, and these cross-links often indicate moments of creativity.

STEPS OF CONCEPT MAPPING IN EDUCATION

Concept mapping helps people to think more effectively as a group without losing their individuality. It helps groups to manage the complexity of their ideas without trivializing them or losing detail.

A concept mapping process involves six steps that can take place in a single day or can be spread out over weeks or months depending on the situation.

1. Preparation Step-There are three things done here. The facilitator of the mapping process works with the initiator(s) (i.e., whoever requests the process initially) to identify who the participants will be. A mapping process can have hundreds or even thousands of stakeholders participating, although we usually have a relatively small group of between 10 and 20 stakeholders involved. Second, the initiator works with the stakeholders to develop the focus for the project. For instance, the group might decide to focus on defining a program or treatment. Alternatively, they might choose to map all of the outcomes they might expect to see as a result. Finally, the group decides on an appropriate schedule for the mapping.

2.Generation Step - The stakeholders develop a large set of statements that address the focus. For instance, they might generate statements that describe all of the specific activities that will constitute a specific social program. Alternatively, they might generate statements describing specific outcomes that might occur because of participating in a program. A wide variety of methods can be used to accomplish this including traditional brainstorming, brain writing, nominal group techniques, focus groups, qualitative text analysis, and so on. The group can generate up to 200 statements in a concept-mapping project.

3.Structuring Step - The participants do two things. First, each participant sorts the statements into piles of similar ones. Most times, they do this by sorting a deck of cards that has one statement on each card. However, they can also do this directly on a computer by dragging the statements into piles that they create. They can have as few or as many piles as they want. Each participant names each pile with a short descriptive label. Second, each participant rates each of the statements on some scale. Usually the statements are rated on a 1-to-5 scale for their relative importance, where a one means the statement is relatively unimportant compared to all the rest, a 3 means that it is moderately important, and a 5 means that it is extremely important.

4. Representation Step – Representation step is where the analysis has done -- this is the process of taking the sort and rating input and "representing" it in map form. There are two major statistical analyses that are used. The first -- multidimensional scaling -- takes the sort data across all participants and develops the basic map where each statement is a point on the map and statements that were piled together by more people are closer to each other on the map. The second analysis -- cluster analysis -- takes the output of the multidimensional scaling (the point map) and partitions the map into groups of statements or ideas, into clusters. If the statements describe activities of a program, the clusters show how these can be grouped into logical groups of activities. If the statements are specific outcomes, the clusters might be viewed as outcome constructs or concepts.

5. Interpretation Step - The facilitator works with the stakeholder group to help them develop their own labels and interpretations for the various maps.

6. Utilization Step – utilizing step involves using the maps to help address the original focus. On the program side, the maps can be used as a visual framework for operational zing the program. On the outcome side, they can be used as the basis for developing measures and displaying results.

ROLE OF LEARNERS/STUDENTS IN USE OF CONCEPT MAPPING IN EDUCATION

- Organize and structure new material
- Increase learning by relating new and old knowledge

- Map out relationships between things such as vocab words, characters in a story, events in history, etc.
- Plan/outline writing projects
- Design their own representations of knowledge
- Brainstorm new ideas
- Take notes
- Create study guides
- Design complex structures
- Plan curriculum
- Assess understanding or diagnose misunderstanding of students
- Explain complex ideas
- Assist struggling readers
- Give a focus question to get the wheels turning.
- Create a parking lot (list of key concepts) to help students determine what to include in their map.
- Provide expert skeleton maps so students have a structure to follow. These are small concept maps started by an expert on the topic, which students can then expand upon.
- Concept maps are especially useful as evaluation tools. For example, instructors can have students create a concept map at the beginning of the semester to assess existing knowledge. Students can then repeat this activity throughout the semester so both students and teachers can evaluate what is being learned. It helps to assess cognitive ability, as deciding what cross-links are most important to include requires high cognitive performance. This activity can also be used to identify and remedy misconceptions students might have.

- Research indicates that students working in small groups and cooperating while learning results in positive cognitive and affective outcomes. Concept mapping allows for this productive small group work among students and teachers in any subject matter.

- Teachers can use concept maps as a pre-reading strategy by inviting students to share what they already know about a particular concept. While reading, teachers should ask students to help add to the map as a group using an overhead or large chart. This provides a visual aid for building upon their prior knowledge with new information they have gathered from reading.

- Teachers may wish to have students practice writing skills by asking students to write on their own concept map.

- Teach vocabulary words explicitly and use simple words.

- Be sure the pointed part of each arrow is clear. Design the graphics to minimize directional confusion.

- When applicable, allow students to draw pictures or use cut out pictures as well as words.

BENEFITS/IMPORTANCE OF CONCEPT MAPPING IN EDUCATION

- Helping students brainstorm and generate new ideas
- Encouraging students to discover new concepts and the propositions that connect them
- Allowing students to more clearly communicate ideas, thoughts and information
- Helping students integrate new concepts with older concepts
- Enabling students to gain enhanced knowledge of any topic

and evaluate the information

- Helps visual learners grasp the material (however all learners benefit from the activity)
- Helps students see relationships between ideas, concepts, or authors
- Utilizes the full range of the left and right hemispheres of the brain
- Helps memory recall
- Helps to clarify and structure ideas
- Aids in developing higher-level thinking skills (create, analyse, evaluate)
- Helps students synthesize and integrate information, ideas and concepts
- Encourages students to think creatively about the subject
- Let us students do self-evaluation of beliefs, values, socialization, etc.
- Helps students evaluate assumptions.
- Provide students with nonlinear visual ways to understand, produce, and represent knowledge.
- Help develop higher-order thinking skills including analytical skills.
- Facilitate the recall and processing of information.
- Help students externalize their knowledge and show their understanding.
- Make explicit structural forms of knowledge and relationships between concepts and therefore enhance student's comprehension.
- They attend to different learning styles.

- They engage students in meaningful learning activities.
- They are effective organizational tools students can use to organize their knowledge.
- Visual representations of knowledge are proved to both stimulate and increase brain activity.
- Boost social interaction, communication and collaborative teamwork.
- They can be used in different content areas and with students from different grades.

IMPLICATIONS OF CONCEPT MAPPING STRATEGY IN CLASSROOM

When created correctly and thoroughly, <u>concept mapping</u> is a powerful way for students to reach high levels of cognitive performance. A concept map is also not just a learning tool, but also an ideal evaluation tool for educators measuring the growth of and assessing student learning. As students create concept maps, they reiterate ideas using their own words and help identify incorrect ideas and concepts; educators are able to see what students do not understand, providing an accurate, objective way to evaluate areas in which students do not yet grasp concepts fully.

Since students might not know how to create a concept map, it is beneficial to model the process in class. Once students understand the process, you can use concept maps in the following ways:

1.Use as an in class pre-assessment - Prior to discussing a topic, ask students to create a concept map. Then, as you discuss the information, they can add to or modify their map to reflect their understanding about the topic.

2. Do as a small group activity - Give your students a problem, case study, or question about a key concept. Divide them into small groups of 4-5 students. Have each group create a concept map as they analyse and synthesize previously learned information into this new scenario. Have the groups present their conclusions.

3. Do as a whole class activity - As a class, create a concept map and use it as a springboard to discuss relationships among the concepts and ideas listed in the map.

4. Fill in the blanks - Before class, create a concept map of the material you want to cover in class. Then, remove some of the concepts and labels. Show the partially completed map to the class and have them fill in the blank spots and label the relationships.

CHAPTER SEVEN

TEAM TEACHING: COLLABARATIVE APPROACH OF TEACHING METHODOLOGY

Dr. Shaila P. Chavan,

Professor,

Adv. V. G. Hande College of Education,

Nashik

CONCEPT AND MEANING OF TEAM TEACHING

Team teaching method is one of the greatest innovations in the teaching sector. The Team Teaching idea originated in USA in 1954 and it found its way to develop courses and teaching strategies. It is a good innovation in teaching strategies.

In simple words, team teaching strategies are simplest form where all teachers of a subject collectively teach a class in that subject. There are some definitions by educationists.

Team teaching is also called collaborative teaching or co teaching strategy. It is used for different subjects especially in middle grades with the help of different teaching method. To provide supportive environment, there are teams of two or four teachers working collaboratively to prepare lesson plans.

As the name suggests it is a group of teachers, working as a team and teaching. The team can range from 2 to 5 teachers who will teach the same group of students.

Definitions of Team Teaching:

1. **Spanish** -"Team teaching is a type of instructional organization involving teaching personnel and the students assigned to them in which two or more teachers are given responsibility, looking together, for all or a significant part of the instruction for some group students".

2. **By Educationist** -"In this teaching strategy two or more than two teachers involve to make a plan of any given subject, or subjects cooperatively, carry it out, and always evaluate its effect on the students periodically".

3. **David Warwick** -"It is a form of organization in which individual teachers decide to pool resources, interest and expertise in order to device and implement a scheme of work suitable to the needs for their pupils and the facilities of their school".

4. **Davis (1995)** -"All arrangements that include two or more faculty in some level of collaboration in the planning and delivery of a course".

CHARACTERISTICS/IMPORTANCE OF TEAM TEACHING

1. **Economic Factors** - It is traditional teaching, if a film is shown to six sections, it is projected six times. This method would organize one or two shows and thus economize use of projector, bulbs, electricity and energy of the teachers.

2. **Structuring in the Enthusiasm** - We teach those topics of the syllabus the best which we known bets and for which we have a liking. This enthusiasm of the teacher is structured by say factual lessons in few large senior groups with adequate follow up in smaller groups.

3. **Development of Staff** - How do we deploy the teachers in brain teaching? The deployment of teachers is done according to areas and methods in which they feel most at home.

4. **Experience Cantered Work** - it means realistic field work of all kinds is undertaken on some afternoons and two or more members of the staff are involved in one project.

5. The team teaching method is flexible

6. In team teaching, teachers need to decide their activities by themselves

7. It is a collective responsibility

8. In team teaching, the whole responsibility is on all the teachers

9. The requirements of pupils, schools and other things are also considered

10. Teaching and evaluation had both done on the co-operative basis

TYPES OF TEAM TEACHING

Team Teaching includes a number of different approaches. Some of the more common are as following

1. Interactive Team Teaching – two faculty members present in front of the class simultaneously.

2. Rotational format Team Teaching – faculty alternate teaching the class. This rotational format has a number of variations depending on the subject matter and the number of faculty involved.

3. Participant-observer Team Teaching – all participating faculty are present for all the classes, but only one is "teaching" at a time. Roles that the other teachers could play as participating observer(s) are model learner, observer, panel member, or resource.

4. Team Coordination – faculty arrange and integrate a

curriculum so as to maximize learning and connections using paired or linked courses, an integrated cluster of independent courses, or freshman interest groups. However, not necessarily team teaching per se, this curriculum-level approach to interdisciplinary can help to achieve some of the expected gains of team teaching.

5. Hierarchic Team Teaching -This type of team teaching method is just similar to a pyramid where different levels of teachers are organized in a structure from top to bottom. The team leader has placed at the top, mid-level teachers just below the team leader and normal teachers at the bottom.

6. Synergetic Team Teaching -In this type of teaching method, there is no differentiation between teachers. Through the cooperation of two or more teachers working together, synergetic team teaching groups can be formed.

OBJECTIVES OF TEAM TEACHING

The team teaching method has practised mainly at a single classroom or space and it has developed to improvise the learning strategies for the students.

1. Improve the quality of the instructions provided.

2. Effective teaching methods as per the interests of the pupils.

3. Make the best usage of abilities, interests and expertise in the teacher's community.

ADVANTAGES/BENEFITS OF TEAM TEACHING

1. Low Cost

One can get an efficient form of learning at a very low cost; as such no new resources are required to start team teaching.

2. Support to Teachers

Many a time, teachers have overburdened with the fact that they have to complete the curriculum by the end of the term, even if they have creative ideas to teach students they do not have enough time to plan and impart the same to the students. Moreover, it can also happen that teachers have ideas but need guidance to develop the skill and impart the same to the students. Team teaching eliminates such problems and other problems of similar kind. When teachers collaborate, they could play on their strengths and weaknesses and together as a team can make a successful way to teach and learn.

3. Closer Integration of Staff

Very often teachers in schools and colleges lack bonding and friendship among themselves. Even worse, a competitive environment has seen among the teachers. The main motive of educational institutes is to impart value to students and work as a whole for being efficient knowledge importers. Envy or competition among teachers can have a negative impact on the Institute and on the student's mind. With team teaching, teachers are bound to bond, as frequent discussions and planning make them develop a good relation. A happy staff can effectively inculcate the vision of Institute

4. Variety of Ideas

When teachers come together with their teaching style, ideas and expertise come together, if planned perfectly, the mixture of best ideas and styles will put forth many ways out of a single topic. It thus helps in better learning

5. Better Involvement of Students

A new method is always appealing; students might wonder what new thing they are going to learn. A team of teacher will have various ways and ideas to put forth, which make the students, put on their thinking cap and question **'why'** for all things. They will come up with various questions, queries and ideas. A dynamic discussion session will increase student's involvement and thus helps in bringing out the best in students

6. Mental Simulation to Students

In traditional lecture only one teacher is teaching, the ideas, thoughts are only one-way. Often students have forced to accept whatever taught and they do not bother to think the other way around. Team teaching helps them question the theories and facts. When the students are very involved it brings out the creativity and the habit of questioning things.

7. Breaks Traditional Lecture Boredom

Let us be very honest, in lectures we are often distracted, either chatting with our friends or checking our phones. On the other hand, maybe jotting down notes, in all the mentioned cases we are giving divided attention. An interactive session, debates, help of visual aids and the like evokes interests among students. Team teaching exactly does that.

8. Better Bonding between Student and Teacher

Humans bond when they interact, it is as simple as that. The bonding has increased when teachers often ask questions and listens to what students have to say. People when heard and appreciated, will ultimately be more engaged.

9. Provokes Participation/Interaction

Teachers will often find students who rarely participate in any activity and are aloof; mostly students with shy personality will not speak much in class. However, during team teaching a variety of ideas has put forth. A perfectly planned lecture will provoke even the most notorious and most aloof people to be engaged. Team teaching helps teachers deal with students of all personalities well and get better engagement

10. Imparts the lesson of Team Management

When students see the way teachers work in team, they indirectly get the lesson of team management and the importance of working in a team. Everyone in their career will need to work in teams. Students get to see how teachers capitalize on each of their strengths how they respect each other's ideas and how as a whole they put the best picture forward. Indirectly, team teaching is helping reduce the extra lecture of team management.

11. Develops Interpersonal Skills and Logic of Students

Students' interaction and logic has improved drastically as they learn to question things and learn how to communicate their ideas effectively. While in case of a debate, students get to learn how to respect the contradicting ideas, accept them and also tell their own thoughts in return.

12. Teachers can give Individual Attention

When a teacher is teaching solely, he or she cannot give attention to the students who has problem learning. The focus is to make the whole group of student understand at a same time. However, we all know that all students are different and everyone has their own learning pace. In team teaching, if one teacher is speaking the other one can solve the queries student raises, without disturbing the whole class.

13. Staff Development

There is no limit to learning, provided if one wishes to, team teaching gives teachers an opportunity to learn and grow themselves. Teachers also get a chance to brush up their skills, work up to their fullest potential and along with that their creativity, motivation and <u>team management skills</u> get a solid boast too.

14. Long-term Knowledge Retention

With a dynamic and interactive session, students have engaged and they learn better. The knowledge retention is much higher than the traditional learning approach

DISADVANTAGES/LIMITATIONS OF TEAM TEACHING

1. Acceptance of Change by Teachers

Let us face it, we humans dislike change, Teachers may not accept the idea of team teaching, they are often rigid and want to stick to the traditional teaching techniques. The idea that they will have to put extra effort and work hard makes them reluctant. Team teaching can only be effective if teachers are willing and happy to involve in the new form of teaching. A forced approach is bound to fail. While traditional teaching has been an attempted and-tried technique, likewise it has disadvantages of traditional teaching; especially nowadays the innovation has improved adapting, more fun and intelligent.

2. Rigidity in Teachers

Apart from accepting the change in form of teaching, teachers often have the rigidity to accept and adjust with other teachers, while <u>working in a team</u> we have to accept others idea and drop ours. Teachers should not have ego and should handle criticism openly.

3. Bad Team Management

Internal coordination and good team tempo is extremely important, internal conflict may result to a complete failure.

4. Personality Conflict

People with contradicting personality must devise a way to work together effectively. A dominating person will overpower other people, a collaborative approach will help everyone grow and devise an effective process of team teaching.

5. Inability to Complete Curriculum

While devising creative curriculum & engaging students in an interactive session, the curriculum may fall behind. Though creative teaching is necessary, it is also important for completing the course syllabus. This is one of the major challenges faced during team teaching.

6. Time for Co-ordination and Planning

Teachers have to take out time from their busy schedules and sit together to devise the lecture flow and activities that have to be carried out. Many times you could find them juggling through their own work and the time required for planning out the course

7. Hard to Keep Track

The sessions at times can get super interactive and teachers will forget the link. The teachers have shared responsibility and have an individual role to play. If anyone of the teachers is absent for some reason then the whole session will be jeopardized.

8. Going Overboard

While being creative and lining up to many activities, it could get way beyond the required amount. A little simulation to student's brain will bring the best in them, but if it gets too much they will find it too hard to comprehend. One needs to find the right amount.

9. Resistance from Students

Since childhood, students get used to the traditional form of teaching, they like the structure and the repetitiveness of the lectures. Most probably they have devised their own ways to make it work, a sudden change in the style of teaching will make them confused and they might resist the change. Some Students like the basic lecture and then they do their self-study to learn in deep about it. You could find students coming up with specific problems that they find difficult. Teaching them everything in detail and inculcating activity, debate or different methods to teach a same topic may make them feel that their time have being wasted.

10. Takes Time to Develop

This new teaching style is fresh to students as well as teachers. Teachers would not have perfect coordination at the first go; they will have to do many trails for reaching a most effective format. There can be an overlap of ideas among teachers or they could not impart whatever they thought of. It could also happen that they overestimated or underestimated the time required to complete the planned tasks. If one of the teachers finds it too difficult to carry out and opts out of it then the whole team will be disrupted. Teachers can also face resistance from the students. Too many ideas and discussion will make the classroom chaotic. Patience from teachers as well as students is required for a successful team teaching

11. Expectation of Higher Compensation

If we compare the efforts required for teaching solely with the efforts required to teach in a team, then the later one is undoubtedly much harder and would require deep study, time and planning. Thus, teachers may demand a higher salary. It could ultimately bring financial pressure on the educational institute.

NECESSARY SKILLS REQUIRED IN THE TEAM OF TEACHERS

1. A team of teachers with a various set of skills prospective and expertise.

2. Vision and sense of direction.

3. Ability to coordinate internally.

4. Excellent team planning.

5. Friendly nature and ability to keep the environment conducive.

TIPS TO MAKE TEAM TEACHING EFFECTIVE

1. Teachers and students must be open to change and must embrace this new form of learning.

2. An effective strategy is necessary which requires undivided attention and time, willingness to <u>make the learning effective</u>. The strategy should involve coverage of course syllabus, activities and quizzes to be carried out, a flow of lecture and documenting and developing a database of the same.

3. Regular meetings and follow up.

4. Rotation of roles to enhance learning and reduce boredom.

5. An effective way to <u>assess students' performance</u>.

6. Respecting others idea.

7. Training to new teachers who are new to the concept of team teaching.

REFERENCES

1. Harris, S. A., and K. J. Watson, 1997. "Small Group Techniques: Selecting and Developing Activities Based on Stages of Group Development." To Improve the Academy.

2. Letterman, M. R., and K. B. Dugan, 2004. "Team Teaching a Cross-Disciplinary Honors Course: Preparation and Development." College Teaching.

3. McDaniel, E. A., 1987. "Faculty Collaboration for Better

Teaching: Adult Learning Principles Applied to Teaching Improvement." In To Improve the Academy: Resources for Student, Faculty and Institutional Development, ed. J. Kurfiss. Stillwater, OK: New Forums Press.

4. McDaniels, E. A., and G. C Colarulli, 1997. "Collaborative Teaching in the Face of Productivity Concerns: The Dispersed Team Model." Innovative Higher Education 22(1).

5. McLaughlin, M. W., and J. E. Talbert. 1993. Contexts that Matter for Teaching and Learning: Strategic Opportunities for Meeting the Nation's Education Goals. Palo Alto, CA: Stanford Center for Research on the Context of Secondary School Teaching.